Simply
Communicate

Kristel Keys Running

DEDICATION

To Adam and my girls,

with more love than you can imagine.

CONTENTS

Acknowledgments   i

1   Communication Roots   1

2   Knowing Why   Pg 9

3   Messaging Successfully   Pg 18

4   Communication Fails   Pg 28

5   The Other Side   Pg 43

6   Getting to Know You   Pg 55

7   Internal Communications   Pg 62

8   External Communications   Pg 69

9   Communication Tools   Pg 73

10   Customer Service   Pg 88

11   What's Next   Pg 99

ACKNOWLEDGMENTS

First and foremost, a thank you to my loving husband Adam and darling daughters for always supporting me and allowing me time to make this book possible. My parents for always being there for me, especially in the most difficult times. Thank you to my college professors along the way for encouraging me to keep going with compliments and praise. Many of my colleagues for collaborating with me and allowing me to learn and grow. My editor Laura for her attention to detail and comments that helped make this book what it is.

1 COMMUNICATION ROOTS

I have been lucky enough to grow up as the world's communications tools also grew up. While I wasn't around for the invention of the telephone or typewriter, these two communication tools (along with handwritten, mailed letters) had only minor improvements in the first 100 years compared to the vast improvements in the more recent 30 years.

When I was just a tiny child, typewriters, not computers and printers, were used to type papers and letters. Many mistakes were made, paper was wasted, and whiteout was expended by the gallons. Keys would stick and typewriters would jam, and the majority of the time was not spent typing, but rather fixing the machine and the mistakes.

In the 80s and 90s, I had two phones in my house, one

downstairs and one upstairs, which were attached to the wall with cords. They were rotary phones, so I would have to dial each number and then wait for the dial to finish its circle until moving onto the next number. There was no caller ID or voicemail, so no one knew who was calling when the phone rang, and there was always excitement to see whom it would be. I had a family phone number that all my family members shared. If I wanted to call someone I would dial his or her number, which I'd memorized, and wait in anticipation for someone to pick up. Because the number was shared, I had to ask for the person I wanted to speak to and hope they were available. If they weren't available, I would leave a message with the person answering the call to have them call me back. I trusted the message was written down correctly and passed onto the appropriate person. Because the phone was attached to the wall, there was no such thing as a private conversation.

I sent and received handwritten letters in the mail. Cursive was the writing style that many used when writing letters. Corresponding with someone took several days or weeks. I remember learning to write in cursive in second grade and thought all the loops and curls were fun to write with. I wrote in cursive frequently as it was required to do on papers and it was also a fancier way of writing than print. Anything that was extra special was written in cursive. I had frilly, girly stationary and cards. Birthdays, anniversaries, and other life events were celebrated with cards. It was always exciting to send and receive mail; even though it took a long time, it was worth the wait. Communication was fun, yet slow, and patience was required.

As I aged, communication tools evolved as technology advanced. Typewriters turned into word processors and then computers. Computers were expensive for personal use, but word processors were more affordable. They were a huge improvement from typewriters because you could type a whole sentence and see it on a digital screen before pressing print. While they weren't as efficient as computers, they were a step in the right direction and greatly appreciated by students typing papers. I remember my first time using one when I was in middle school. I was writing a paper for class and instead of getting the typewriter out, I just plugged in the word processor, turned it on, put the paper in and typed a sentence. I could see the letters pop up on a screen before my eyes and could catch any typos before they hit the paper. Of course there were occasional errors, but a lot were caught before the words were printed onto the paper. Once I was satisfied with what I typed, I hit the print button and the line was printed. I would then move onto the next sentence.

The first computer I used was in the late 80s in elementary school. It was an Apple IIe, complete with the black screen and green writing. Schools were lucky enough to have a couple of computers, and children would take turns using them. Floppy disks allowed us to save our work, so a person could come back at a later time and finish without losing everything. Eventually one or two computers turned into entire computer labs at school. If you were lucky, you had a computer at home, but I didn't know many people in the early 90s with home computers.

Phones went from rotary to push buttons and eventually cordless. I watched the evolution of the phone, and when we got our first push button phone, I was ecstatic. I thought it was so cool that I could just push a button to call someone, instead of dialing a number and waiting for each round to take place before I could go onto the next number. It was so fast, and I really liked the sound each button made as I pressed them. When we got our first cordless phone, I thought we were very technologically advanced. The first cordless phones didn't work very well however, and I couldn't walk too far away from the base unit, or I'd lose the call. The call quality was a little scratchy, too. None of that mattered though, because having a cordless phone was too exciting for anyone to care if it worked well or not. Few people had car phones in the early 90s; they were mostly for business purposes. I remember my older sister had one and while it was state of the art back then, it was huge and cumbersome compare to what is available today.

In the late 90s things really began to change. Computers were able to connect to the Internet, albeit at dial up speed. Email was born, as well as instant messaging or chat. Car phones turned into cell phones and became more popular. Finally computer screens went from large square boxes to thin and rectangular. Internet speeds increased, social media sites popped up here and there, cell phones turned into texting machines, and eventually smart phones came and could connect to the Internet, be a camera, play music, and more.

Today an excess of communication tools exist and can be used instantly. Patience is not required. Finding ways to communicate is becoming increasingly easier and faster. Information and communication is everywhere, and we are faced with too much information. We must learn to filter out what is important and necessary for us to know and ignore or remove what isn't. Communication and all the tools available have become time consuming and difficult to navigate. Staying on top of it all can be nearly impossible in this busy world.

I am glad that I was able to experience the changes in

technology and communication. It gives me a greater appreciation of what we have today, and I occasionally yearn for the quieter, slower times of yesteryear. When a person understands communication and the tools used, it aids in communication efforts.

I am certain that my experience watching communication evolve over the years led me to my love for it. I pursued a communications degree for my undergraduate and then sought out employment in the field. After working for various companies throughout the years I have learned even more about communicating in business and the problems that were faced. In addition to my professional experience with communication I also deal with communication in my personal life on a daily basis with my family. I have two daughters, a baby and an eight-year-old, and my husband that I need to effectively communicate with to make sure our household functions properly.

Communication problems exist in nearly every company. Some of the most common complaints include employees confused about who they need to communicate with, timeliness of communication efforts and departments not wanting to share information with other departments. There are also complaints of receiving too much information. How many times have you received an email that was way too long or had a conversation with someone that seemed never ending; maybe the person just rambled on and on and kept repeating themselves. We will talk more about communication problems in chapter four.

This book is intended to teach you what you can do to have effective communication at your company. I hope you will be able to model the way and influence others to be better communicators. In order to have effective communication, you and your employees need to take it seriously and put in an effort to be successful. Communication should be a priority, and you should make time to do it. You want your employees to work better together, and this book will teach you how to communicate respectfully, while creating trust and empathy. You will learn how employees impact, support, and interact with each other, and you will learn if what you are currently doing is the best way for it to be done or if there are other tools you should be using instead.

This book will give you a solid foundation to provide training to your employees so they won't say, "I don't know how to communicate effectively" or "I don't know what's expected of me." Training your employees on effective communication will set expectations and create consistency in how they communicate with each other companywide.

We will cover the following topics in this book. Upon completion you should have a strategic plan in place on how to effectively communicate and watch your business become even more successful, filled with satisfied employees and customers.

1. Being clear and concise
2. Clarity of who needs what and when
3. Communication tools
4. Communication problems
5. Knowing your audience

Think about it

Remember a time when you experienced really poor communication. What would you change about the interaction?

Activity

Write down what you hope to achieve by the end of this book.

2 KNOWING WHY

We all talk and we all write: but does that make us all expert communicators? There must be something more to communication than the words that are coming out if there are college degrees dedicated to communication and job titles with the word communication in them. What skills are involved with communication? Knowing that effective communication is more than just words is a start.

Communication is a buzzword that is not going away. In nearly every job description, having the ability to communicate effectively is a requirement. People are social creatures, and in order to work effectively as part of a team, they need to be able to communicate with each other. Regardless if you are communicating internally or externally - everything we do is connected in some shape or another. What does it mean to communicate, and why does it matter?

The true definition of communicate is the following: "To share or exchange information, news, or ideas." In business, the definition can be somewhat vague and leaves employees searching for a clearer sense of what is expected. Employees struggle to communicate with their bosses, managers struggle to communicate with their employees, employees struggle to communicate with each other and with customers, and customers struggle to communicate back to the company. Why is it so difficult to communicate successfully in business? Are we not able to share or exchange information, news, or ideas in a professional setting, or are the parameters just too ambiguous?

Some people make the mistake of disseminating massive amounts of information because they feel the more, the better. They end up trying to find out all the information they possibly can and share all the information they have. This ends up being counter-effective because the information is not being filtered or shared appropriately, and it turns into white noise that employees ignore. Employees are busy and realistically do not have the time to listen to every bit of information available in the company.

Other people are too selective in their communication efforts. They over-filter information that is disbursed because they don't think other people need to know about it, which can create a silo mentality. When employees feel like they aren't getting all the information needed to do their job, they feel left out and resent the people or departments withholding the information. When important information isn't being shared, everyone in the company suffers, including the customers and sales. This happened at a previous company I worked for. The department was so busy working on their own stuff, they forgot it was important to share information with the rest of the company on what they were working on, what products were in hot demand and short in supply. Customers started calling the consumer relations line complaining about this department because they weren't getting their needs met, products were getting delivered and no one was letting them know what was going on. Sales decreased because other departments weren't able to step in and help find more product and more customers because no one was aware of the situation.

The key is to find the happy medium in information broadcasting, where less is more because it's the right information. If you have a situation where there is either too much or too little communicating happening, there are ways to solve the problem. The five most important things to consider when communicating effectively are:

1. Who is your audience?
2. What does your audience want to know?
3. What key messages do you want to get out?
4. Where will your audience find your information/products?
5. What's in it for them?

Don't worry if you can't answer those questions off the top of your head; I will walk you through each step. Remember, no matter how great your product or service is, if no one knows about it, no one wins.

Who is your audience?

When communicating effectively, you must know your audience. This rule is applicable to business as well as personal interactions. If you aren't connecting positively with your audience, then your communication will not be successful. When determining whom your audience is, you will need to ask yourself a series of questions.

1. Is your audience internal or external?
2. What are their demographics?
3. Do you have more than one target audience?

Once you have determined who your audience is, you must start to get to know them. We will go into this in-depth in chapter six.

What does your audience want to know?

Based on your research and findings in determining who your audience is, you will be closer to figuring out what your audience wants to know. You will discover what is important to them and why it's important to them. When you know these details, communicating with your audience will be simple. You will be able to take massive amounts of information and filter it so that it makes sense and is applicable to their jobs and lives. Your audience will start listening to the messages being sent to them and will respond positively in the way you want them to.

What key messages do you want to get out?

Now that you know whom your audience is and what they want to know, you can focus on your messages. What are the key messages you hope to disseminate? If you are hoping to tell your audience about a new promotion or product, think carefully about the most important things you want to say. There may be ten to twenty really important points, but you only have your audience's attention for a short while, so you need to focus on the most important ones. This is where being strategic in your communications is really important and where you merge your key messages with what your audience wants to hear to make the most powerful impact. We dive deeper into messaging in chapter three.

Where will your audience find your information/products?

As you can see, knowing your audience is vital to having successful communications. After all, without them you would have no customers and therefore no business. Knowing who your audience is and what they want to know is important, but you must advertise in the appropriate places, so your audience will discover you and your products. This part goes hand in hand with knowing your audience, and one step in knowing your audience is knowing their habits: what they read, where they hang out, what they listen to. If you know those answers, you will be able to target those specific places with your messaging. If you don't know the answers, you will discover them in the research conducted when getting to know your audience.

This is why we devote an entire chapter to knowing your audience. It is really quite important in marketing and communicating, and unfortunately many companies get so consumed with their products and what they have to say that they completely forget about their audience and what their audience needs to hear.

What's in it for them?

You know your audience. Check. You understand what your audience wants to know. Check. You know your key messages to stay in tune with your audience's demands. Check. Your audience can find your information and products. Check.

All the pieces seem to be falling into place, but we can't forget the final question: what's in it for them? How is this product or service going to benefit their life? Why should they care? These questions should hopefully be covered in your key messages, but if not, you will want to jump into your target audiences shoes and figure out how what you have will fit into their lives, how they will benefit from it. This may be a very simple and obvious answer or it may take some digging, thinking, and strategizing.

The most important thing to remember is your audience. Study them, follow them, become as close to them as possible so you can do your job effectively and connect with them and build relationships and loyalty.

Why does communication matter to a business? Communication (or lack thereof) determines how people work together internally and how the public views them externally. Communication is prevalent in all aspects of business, which is what makes it so significant. Without proper communication, no one would know what is expected of them, why they are doing, the things they are doing, what the next steps are, what products and initiatives are coming up, why to buy a product, etc. The list goes on and on.

Think of it this way. I have this awesome business selling the cure for the common cold over on State Street. It's something everyone wants, but I don't communicate my business to anyone. No one knows it exists. So I sit in this store day in and day out, alone. No one stops in, no one calls, no one writes. I don't sell any products because no one knows about the business. I can't grow because I am not selling anything. I can't hire anyone because no one knows about the business. Without communications a business will fail and will fail quickly. Even some communication is better than none, but what you really want is effective communication so you can be successful!

Think about it

When starting a strategic plan it is important to know why communication matters at your company. Think about what you are trying to achieve with communication efforts.

Activity

Write down why you want to have effective communication at your company. Then answer the five most important things to consider when communicating effectively. *(If you can't answer each of these fully, don't worry- we will address each of these individually throughout the book. Just answer the best you can for now).*

1. Who is your audience?
2. What does your audience want to know?
3. What key messages do you want to get out?
4. Where will your audience find your information/products?
5. What's in it for them?

3 MESSAGING SUCCESSFULLY

Messaging is very similar to communicating, and some may use the two words interchangeably.
Communicating is the act of sharing information, and messaging is the art of saying the information in the way you want to say it. Messaging is about being in control of your communication efforts. Messaging is the part of communication that can mean success or failure. What you say should be determined by the needs of the audience, not the needs of the company. Messaging is an art that takes practice. Just like there are positive and negative ways to communicate, there are positive and negative ways to message. A successful business will be consistent in their messaging, but what does that mean?

In this day and age of information overload, consistent

messaging is more important than ever. Some may think that it means saying the same thing over and over again, which can be true sometimes. A company must strive to have the same tone on important subjects, and everything the public sees must look similar and ultimately stand for the same thing. If you have numerous different looks, inconsistent placements of logos, a variety of fonts, and messages that say one thing one day and another the next, you could be confusing your customers and turning them away.

Still there are a lot of business owners asking if messaging is really that important. If you think the answer is no, you are wrong. Messaging is essential and provides an opportunity to turn a not-so-good situation into a positive one.

At a previous job I worked with farmers and there was a less than ideal year for crops. Many farmers were losing production because of the quality of crops they were feeding their cattle. In order to help the farmers increase production, we had an educational call for them to attend and learn about some things they could do. In messaging this call, we had to keep a positive vibe going so farmers wouldn't be even more discouraged. Instead of messaging to farmers about their poor crops, we told them to join the call to increase production with existing forage. We messaged the call positively and encouraged people, rather than discouraged them. The call was very popular and was the most highly attended in the history of the educational calls. Farmers were appreciative of the support and saw an increase in production and income because of the call and messaging that was done around it.

In most situations, you will want to deliver positive messaging or at least neutral messaging to keep the morale up. Politicians screw this up all the time, especially during campaign season. Instead of listening to their audience, who asks for friendly, positive messaging, they use smear campaigns and tons of negativity and blaming. While this can work in political campaigns, people react negatively when hearing or seeing this type of marketing. According to a Gallup poll from 2000, the American public has little tolerance for negative ads with 57 percent of voters are dissatisfied with the way candidates conduct their campaigns. You don't want your customers to get disgusted every time they hear or see your name or logo. Instead you want to leave them with positive emotions, so they are excited for your products and want more of them.

Messaging effectively is important for maintaining

customer loyalty and for managing your reputation. If your messaging is not well thought out, you could be headed for a disaster. Remember that positivity and honesty go a long way, and honesty trumps positivity every day. If you have a bad situation or information to share, you have to be honest and deliver it. The good news is this can be done in a way that will contain the problem and retain your customers. You can even message honestly while being positive! Messaging the right way takes practice and work, so don't be afraid to work at it and use trial and error. If something doesn't work, try something else. Get other opinions from other people and ask for feedback.

Remembering to use the five W's and one H when messaging will help a lot.

1. Who
2. What
3. Where
4. Why
5. When
6. How

Who

Who needs to know the information you are about to

share? It's important to know who needs to know the information you have. Start a list and make sure you have all the key stakeholders covered. Do your employees need to know, your customers, how about community members? Check the list a few times to make sure you aren't forgetting anyone. You also need to remember whom this message is about. Nine times out of ten it will be about your business or product, but don't forget to mention this in your messaging. Do so in a way that is appealing to the receiver, and don't make it all about you, but rather all about them.

What

What information do you need to share? If communicating internally, you should share information that people need to do their jobs. You might also want to share updates, announcements, data, and expectations. If communicating externally, you should share information that will help sell your products and your company. If a new product is launching, you should share that. If you did some community work, share that too! Remember: if you think someone would be interested or benefit from the information, you should share it. Information is good as long as it meets the needs of the recipient.

Where

Where will the product, event, initiative, or information be for the audience to access it? Telling this to your customers is important because if they can't locate what it is you are messaging about, it won't do either of you any good. You also have to consider where you are going to do the messaging. Will it be at an event, through the mail, on television or radio? Where does your audience hang out, and where is the best location to reach them?

Why

Why do you need to communicate the information, and why does the audience care? A lot of people forget the second part and forget about why the audience should care about the information. You usually need to communicate something to inform. You might want to increase sales or just brand awareness, which would both be valid "whys." Why does the audience care? Well, that is when knowing your audience is important. When you know your audience, you will know what is important to them and why they care about your company and your products or services. We will learn more about the audience in chapter six.

When

When does your information need to be communicated? If you communicate information too soon, you could be jumping the gun or announcing confidential information. If you communicate information too late, people get angry because they feel like you were keeping secrets from them or they missed an opportunity. It is important to be timely when communicating so you meet the expectations of your audience. Most of the time information is not communicated soon enough, especially internally, and employees find out in other ways. Be aware if this is happening at your company and consider communicating sooner so resentment doesn't build. If you have an event or initiative taking place or a product that will be available or on sale, you will need to let your audience know when these thing are happening and consider the date for communication so it is prior to the event or sale.

How

How will you communicate your information? There are a number of communication tools available; see chapter nine for an in-depth look at them. Remember to be clear and concise in your communication efforts and use a respectful tone. Knowing your audience will help determine which tools to use. Let the audience know how this information will affect them. Will it make their life easier? Will they be more successful? When you tell the customer how they will benefit from the message, they are more likely to listen and to care about it.

Setting the right tone in your communication will ensure your message comes across favorably. Crafting the communication so that it portrays the right message is key for businesses success. Take a look at your current messaging. Do you see any red flags? Are there any parts that could be taken the wrong way or be considered offensive? If you answered yes, you should consider changing your messaging. If you don't know, ask people for their opinions. Ask customers for feedback. Your business will thank you.

One more important aspect of messaging is the ability to be concise. You do not want to lose your audience with too many words that interfere with the message. When crafting your message remember that less is more. The more clear and concise your message is, the more likely you will reach your audience and see the desired results. All too often I see people and businesses trying to lure their audience in by using big, descriptive words, and I'll admit sometimes they are necessary. But people run into problems when they use too many of these fluff words, and the message gets lost, or the audience gets confused. What I recommend doing is practice being concise in every thing you do. Start by trying to introduce yourself with just five words. For example, I would say Kristel, communication expert, mom, wife. Of course, we wouldn't actually communicate like that to each other, but it is a great exercise to do when practicing to be concise. You will soon find there are a lot of fluff words involved when communicating. You'll see what is absolutely necessary and what is not.

Remember messaging takes practice and patience. Getting a great message won't happen on the first try and will take work. People go to school and work on messaging for years, and they still don't get it just right on the first try – so don't get discouraged. Be persistent and find a few people you can bounce ideas off of. Most companies have teams that work on messaging together, so find some trusted friends to give you their honest opinions and constructive feedback.

Think about it

What type of messaging do you want? Think of companies that have messaging you like and try to replicate it, but still be unique to differentiate yourself.

Activity

Find five emails you think could have been more concise. Rewrite them while trying to be as clear and concise as possible, while still keeping the main message. Try writing in bullet points. This will help you pull out the key information and removes all the excess information that may not be necessary. Practice this frequently, and crafting the perfect message will get easier and come more naturally to you.

4 COMMUNICATION FAILS

Every company has communication problems, and in this chapter we look at some common issues that arise frequently and address how to overcome them. Being able to understand the problem is just as important as any other part of communicating.

Communicating effectively can be a difficult task. Every day we hear of communication failures that many companies experience. Every day businesses have problems with their communication efforts, whether they are internal or external. While there are many reasons why communication fails, many of those reasons fall under two main categories:

1. No idea/plan
2. No action

No idea/plan

When a company doesn't know the right way to communicate with their audience, communication efforts will fail. They either don't know their audience, so they don't know how to reach them, or they just don't have a plan for their communication efforts. Once you have an idea of what to do, you should create a plan. A plan is merely something to follow; write down all the steps so you don't forget anything important and stay on task. If you don't have any idea of where to start with communicating, this book should provide you with valuable information and a solid foundation of where to start and knowing your audience.

Even if you have the beginning of a good idea, you will need to turn it into a plan and review it several times with several people to make sure you have met all the criteria I discussed in chapter one. The following is an example of a company that did not do research and did not take the time to get to know their audience and ended with a failed communication effort.

I recently watched a video a company created to recruit people to want to work there. The video was short and to the point and had a great idea behind it. It started out saying that working at this company would provide a rewarding career, which was priceless, but didn't explain why this company was able to provide a rewarding career. Instead it listed some points the company was proud of, but wasn't convincing enough to entice someone to move to a rural area. Unfortunately the video left my mind almost as quickly as it entered and did not do what it was intended to do. It was forgettable because it did not connect with me. Sadly this company thinks it has a really great recruiting video out there, and it doesn't, all because the creator forgot one thing - the audience. Prospective employees who are educated and experienced and do not live in rural Wisconsin would need to have more of an explanation of why the area is so great, what the company offers that they can't get somewhere else and why they should move to this remote location.

No one bothered to ask the important questions of why is this important to the target audience, why do they care, what's in it for them? So what was created was a hurried look at what the company thinks are its selling points. They didn't ask existing employees what makes the company unique or why they chose to work there. They didn't highlight areas that would have been selling points, and the areas they did touch on were rushed through and didn't go into detail about what mattered to prospective employees.

A video that could have had so much potential failed because the right questions weren't asked upfront. Remember that if you have a great idea (and you probably do), you need to carefully implement it, or you will not achieve the results you desire. Always remember your intended audience, because if they don't relate or connect with your communication efforts, it doesn't matter. Don't create something because you like it, but create something because your audience/customers will like it.

No action

In my experience over the years, I have seen a number of great ideas when it comes to communicating with others. Ideas exist, and unfortunately that's where they stay - as ideas - which is exactly what the problem is. Ideas are everywhere on how to improve communication, what steps need to be taken to decrease siloing, and what communication is effective…only those ideas typically go nowhere. Lack of action is the real problem that is keeping many businesses from effective communication. Lack of action happens for several reasons including:

1. Lack of time to implement a plan
2. Lack of knowledge of how to implement a plan
3. Limited resources, such as manpower

Lack of time

If you find your biggest challenge in implementing a communications plan is lack of time, be happy, as this is the easiest problem to solve. Okay, so you might be saying to yourself, I have no time, and there is no more time to add to a day, so how can this be the easiest problem to solve? Simple answer, you make time. Communicating effectively will pay off for years to come and will be well worth the time invested. Schedule a chunk of time, for example an hour a day, to focus on implementing your plan. If that isn't possible, consider hiring someone to do it for you. There are many options available, such as a temporary employee, a contracted employee, or a permanent employee. There are a lot temp agencies around that you can go to and pretty quickly location a temporary employee if you decide that is what you need. Contracted employees can be found by word of mouth, doing a quick search online, or even by going to freelance websites where there are a number of skilled workers available to do whatever job you need. A permanent employee takes a bit more time to locate and secure, as you have to develop a job description, post the job, conduct interviews and then make a decision – however, it is well worth it if you decide you need someone long-term.

If you expect your employees to be good communicators, and communication is in their job description, you need to allow them time to do it. Perhaps one hour each day is dedicated solely to communication efforts. There is no right or wrong answer on how to make time; what's imperative is that you do it. A plan is worthless if it's not being executed.

Lack of knowledge

Lack of knowledge could be not knowing what to do first and it could also be not knowing your audience or what they want. If you don't know your audience, we will cover that in chapter six. Maybe you know your audience and what they want and have a plan, but you don't know what step to take first. If you are unsure of how to implement your plan, take it one step at a time. Think carefully about what it is you don't know and figure out a way you can learn about it. Hopefully this book will help you, and if not, you have other resources you can turn to. You can do some online research, you can hire a consultant, or you can hire a qualified employee to implement your plan. Conducting research online would be the fastest and cheapest route to take if you have time on your hands and have a solid base knowledge of where to begin. A consultant would be ideal if you don't want to deal with the hassle of hiring a permanent employee, but want the vast knowledge and expertise they bring. You can establish a relationship with a consultant and work with them long-term on an as needed basis. This is beneficial if you want someone you know and trust and they understand your business and needs, but don't need as often as a permanent employee. Finally, if you have determined you will need someone on a fairly regular basis and have enough work for a part-time or full-time permanent position, you should hire an employee to work with you on developing and implementing your plan. The same goes for creating a plan. If you aren't sure where to start, choosing one of the options I just listed would be an ideal place to look.

Limited resources

Not having qualified staff, enough staff, or access to the different vehicles you will use can pose a problem. As previously stated, really your only option here is to hire someone. I understand that you might have a tight budget and can't afford to hire another employee to work on your communication plan for you, but don't think of it as hiring an employee as much as investing in your business. Because communication is so important in business, it would do more harm if you ignored your communication needs.

Knowing you have several options, you can and

should choose the best one for your company. Maybe you know that the work to implement your plan will be a lot right away and then not so much after it gets started. It would make more sense to hire a temporary employee or contract work, as you or another employee could take over after the initial work is done. If the work in implementing a plan will remain pretty consistent throughout time, but it isn't enough for a full-time employee, then hiring a permanent, part-time employee would be the wisest choice. And finally, if there is a lot of work to be done, and it's going to be consistent and require someone's constant attention, then hiring a full-time, permanent employee to fill the need is the way to go.

It's unfortunate that so many companies choose not to implement a great idea or plan because they don't have the time, knowledge, or resources. So many people say we'll get to that tomorrow, next week, next month, next year, and then each day goes by without any action. I have seen companies have great ideas sitting around for years because no one took the time to act upon them. In a company I previously worked for there was no companywide strategic communication plan. Each department did whatever they wanted and there was no consistency and no expectations. Many people thought there should be a plan and a lot of people talked about a plan, but no one ever took any action. They were all waiting for someone else to do it, and had many meetings discussing this plan, but a plan wasn't developed or implemented. Morale was low, complaints were rampant, and departments resented one another because of poor communication. If someone had taken the time initially to work on a plan, the company could have been much more productive and successful.

I have witnessed some pretty terrible internal communications efforts - from the company getting bought out and nearly all of the staff losing their jobs only to find out about it a month before it would happen to a CEO getting fired and having no communication to employees about it. I understand that there may be some HR issues with communicating certain things, but seriously show your employees some respect by communicating what you can to them. I still don't understand what went wrong in these scenarios, except that there was no thought put into them.

I am sure the company that got bought out knew well in advance that it was going to happen. Instead of giving employees a month to find a new job, the company should have made an announcement as soon as they were aware and given a timeline of events so employees were empowered to make better decisions.

If any employee decided to leave prior to the company closing, they might not have qualified for the payout, but they would have had more time to find a new job.

When a CEO or any other executive leaves a company, either voluntary or involuntary, it will affect the employees and should be communicated appropriately. When I learned of the CEO getting let go, I asked if it was going to be communicated to the employees. I was told no and was not given an explanation why. They just said they felt like it didn't need to be communicated. Employees found out about it through the rumor mill at the water cooler and it really brought down morale. Employees were confused, worried, and uncertain and anxiety was high. If the company had just communicated to employees right away, they would have alleviated a lot of the anxiety of employees because it wouldn't have looked like the company was trying to hide something.

How you handle a really difficult situation says a lot about your leadership style and how the company is run. If you keep big news a secret or don't communicate it with grace, your employees and the public will think that is how everything is done, and it can really tarnish your reputation. Even if it is just a one-time occurrence, brushing something major under the rug shows that you don't respect the employees.

It's showing that they aren't important enough to be addressed, and it makes you look like a coward for hiding in a corner when negative issues arise.

Don't be the secretive manager who is resented by the employees. Improve your communication and overall morale and productivity in your workplace by communicating effectively. Practice taking negative information and finding the silver lining. Once you get used to messaging negative information it will come more naturally to you. It may never get easy, but you will have experience at doing it.

Another uncomfortable situation I experienced was when a staff member accidently emailed something bad about another employee to them. Before the information got back to me it went to three other managers who kept passing it along. A superior told me that there was no way to fix the problem, and it was a huge crisis. I didn't believe that and thought she was being overly dramatic. Instead of pretending like it didn't happen and ignoring it or brushing it under the rug, I brought the two parties together in a room and addressed it candidly. They were both visibly upset, and it was an uncomfortable situation. However, by addressing the issue immediately and directly, the damage was minimized, and both parties were able to work together and be productive in a much shorter timeframe than if it hadn't been addressed. If the situation was brushed under the rug like my superior had suggested, both employees would have felt uncomfortable around each other and the one who received the email would have had major trust issues. Not just with the employee who sent the email, but also with everyone, because she would think that others might think the same of her. She would have likely avoided people and work wouldn't have gotten completed as she was a support person for the department and good communication was imperative. Communication was the key to solving the problem, but had I listened to my superior it would have been brushed under a rug and would have potentially exploded into a much bigger problem. In that organization, management was clearly afraid of communicating because of employees' reactions.

Communication Problems

Besides major communication failures, there are also communication problems that exist in companies. Some of those problems include:

1. Too much information
2. Too little information
3. Information stagnates

Too much information

Too much information is a direct result of all the newsletters, emails, meetings, etc. Emails that are too long and wordy can lose people's attention quickly like being in a conversation with someone who goes on and on and you can't escape. Too many people are trying to be good communicators, and it just ends up as a bunch of stuff you have to filter through to find the one piece of information you really need. Too much information can waste time, for those disseminating it and those weeding through it. Managers and employees need to learn to be more efficient with their information sharing and take time at the front of sharing, so time isn't wasted in creating and receiving messages.

Too little information

When there isn't enough information that passes onto others, it can cause problems, just as too much information can. Not sharing information, for whatever reason, causes silos amongst departments. It can also cause confusion if information is missing and work may not get completed from the lack of information. Most of the time information isn't withheld on purpose, but rather because employees don't know whom to share it with or who the information will affect.

Information Stagnates

Another problem with communication happens when information stagnates. This can happen with anyone at any time. Information may not trickle down from managers or other people with the information. This can happen because people get so busy and forget to share information. Information also stagnates when there is confusion of who needs to know the information. Sometimes information stagnates when a person wants to feel like they are needed, so they don't share the information with anyone else. When this happens, mistakes get made, and employees feel resentful for not being included or privy to valuable information that they need to do their jobs or that could make their jobs more efficient. Again, just like with too little information, when information stagnates, it's not because people mean to not share, but rather it's generally because they are too busy, or they do not know who needs the information to do their job.

Think about it

Has your company experienced a communication fail? If so, what could you have done differently to prevent it from happening?

Activity

Create a list of communication problems in your company and develop ways to overcome them.

5 THE OTHER SIDE

The other side of communication is quite possibly my favorite, and it is also probably the most forgotten aspect of successful communication. When talking about communications, we often focus on the outgoing information. We want to take as much information as we can and disperse it as widely and quickly as possible. This is important to do, but what's equally important is the other side of communication: the receiving end.

Communication is a two-way street, and you can have the best information all over the place, but if your intended audience isn't receiving it, then the information is virtually worthless. So we are presented with the question of, "How do we get our audience's attention?"

As a mother, I deal with this on a daily basis. I ask my daughter to do something (numerous times), and there is no follow through. When I ask later why it hasn't been done, she explains to me that she didn't hear me. I failed at communicating with her, because the message didn't go through. As a mother, I need to remember to communicate in a way that makes sense to my eight-year-old, not in a way that makes sense to me.

When we communicate digitally (e.g. fax machine, email, phone call) we often get error messages to alert us when messages don't go through. We are fortunate to receive the alert because we know we need to try sending the message again. Once the message is successfully sent, we then must trust that the intended recipient sees the message and interprets it the way we intended. Wouldn't it be great if we received an error message every time a communication effort failed so we could fix it right away? Well, if we play close attention we can see that we do get error messages, but they aren't so obvious. They come in all shapes and sizes, such as low sales, customers leaving or unsatisfied, employees not completing tasks as requested, and so on.

There are ways you can be proactive when waiting to see if the message was received successfully.

1. Feedback
2. Metrics
3. Action

Feedback

One way is to ask for feedback. You can do this by asking customers what their level of satisfaction is, what you can improve on, what you are doing right, etc. Getting this type of information is imperative to successful communication. You are communicating information out, and your customers and employees are communicating information back in. It is up to you to decide how and when you gather that information and what you do with it.

There are several ways to gather feedback. You can have ongoing customer feedback surveys in paper copy and online. You can have targeted surveys given just before and just after a new communication goes out. You can also have a department dedicated to gathering feedback by having a consumer hotline, email address, and/or mailing address.

Metrics

Using metrics is a great way to see if your communication efforts are working. You can track your sales just before and just after the effort to see if there is an increase, decrease, or if they remain steady. You can also track website or store visits to see if they increase, decrease or stay the same. Alternatively, you can watch interaction from phone inquiries, social media and your blog. Metrics can be used for tracking how successful internal communications are by keeping track of work that is completed accurately and timely. If you are asking employees to do a specific task you can watch response rates to see if the communication was effective.

Knowing that successful communication is about both sides will help your communication efforts.

Action

You know your communication efforts are successful when you see action. If your product is moving, if sales are happening, if your phone is ringing - action is taking place. If you see no action you need to rethink your efforts and determine what went wrong and fix the errors. Action is the best way to see if the message was received successfully, especially when you are making sales because it means money in the bank.

The role of trust

Trust plays an important role in successful

communication, and it is deeply tied to the other side of communication. Building trust with your audience is vital to effective communication.

Think about the last time someone lied to you and how you felt. Was it easy to believe them the next time they told you something? It is an age-old fable, but the lessons from the boy who cried wolf are important to remember if you want to be a great communicator. For example, don't constantly tell someone something if you don't mean it. You will lose their trust and when they finally do mean something, they will not believe you. How do you build and maintain trust?

1.   Tell the recipient the truth. This one seems like a no-brainer, but I have seen and experienced the opposite time and time again. People don't want to tell the truth because they are afraid of how the recipient will respond, how it will make them look, or how it will make the company look. If you don't tell the truth, no matter how painful it can be, you will end up paying for it in the long run. When the recipient finds out the truth (*they will, they always do*), they will be more upset with you because you lied to them and broke their trust. Don't tell people what you think they want to hear; opt for the truth in all situations, no matter what.

2.   Follow through with your actions. If you say you

are going to do a specific task by a specific time, you better accomplish it as promised. People overpromise work and other things and then find themselves not being able to meet expectations. Most of the time, you will get a break if it just happens once, but repeat offenders lose credibility and the recipient's trust rapidly. If you are in a bind and can't uphold your end of the deal, let the recipient know as soon as possible and follow the advice of number one. Tell them the truth and give them a new expected date.

3.   Treat people fairly. You are being watched more than you think, and people are constantly judging your behaviors. If you favor one person over another, it will be noticed, and people will lose trust in you. Remember to treat everyone fairly. It doesn't mean you have to treat everyone the same, but you should show respect to everyone and be fair in your interactions. For example, if you have different work locations and one person lives closer to A and one person lives closer to B, then it would be fair to let them each work at the location closest to them. You aren't treating them the same, because if you were they would have to work at the same location, but you are being fair by letting them work at the location that is best for them. Another example is giving two employees projects to work on. If you are always giving projects to one employee and not another, the employee who didn't get projects would feel like they

were treated unfairly. By giving all employees projects you are being fair. Even though they are not working on the same project, they are getting equal amounts of work. In this example, you need to be careful about the type of project you are assigning. If one project is seen as more favorable, for any reason, then the next time projects are assigned; you should give another person the more favorable project.

This point is especially true for people who have direct reports. Favoritism is exceptionally noticeable and causes a lot of damage, particularly when communicating.

These three points are super easy to do, yet people fail to do them on a daily basis. Remember that the key to superior communication is to establish trust first and foremost. It will build your reputation faster than anything else.

Listening

Listening plays an important role in communication. Because most think of communicating as spewing out information, listening doesn't get much attention when focusing on effective communication. To be an awesome communicator, you have to take an active role in listening. Here are some tips on how to improve your listening skills:

1.   Understand the message
2.   Repeat back what was heard
3.   Remove distractions
4.   Acknowledge the speaker
5.   Take responsibility

Understand the message

Oftentimes when we are listening to someone speak, we are half-listening to what they are saying and half-focusing on what our response is going to be. Or worse yet, we aren't listening at all and thinking about something else entirely. When we don't fully listen, the message can get twisted and harm effective communication. Rather than trying to figure out what your response will be, try listening with the sole purpose of understanding the message. Understanding the message is an integral part of effective communication and can get missed on numerous occasions.

When I am talking with my daughter, I want to make sure I understand what she is saying or I want to make sure she understands what I am saying. In either case, I make sure we both stop what we are doing and look each other in the eye, so we are more likely to be listening to the other person and therefore more likely to understand what the other is saying.

Repeat back what was heard

Once the speaker has completed the message, you should repeat back what you heard. This is especially important to do if there was confusion or questions with the messaging. This allows you to tell the speaker what you heard and allows the speaker to gather essential feedback, such as, was the message clear and concise, was enough information provided, was the message received in the intended way, etc.

The speaker can then correct any misinformation when they hear what you heard. Both sides benefit from this step with enhanced communication efforts and increased opportunities to ensure the message was received properly.

Because my daughter is only eight years old, I always make her repeat back to me what I told her, otherwise she will come back later and say she didn't hear me. A simple yes or head nod isn't enough to make sure the message was received as intended. When I implement this step, I find it is much more effective because she is showing she did hear and understand what I said and is more likely to follow through with whatever I asked her to do.

Remove distractions

Having a conversation with someone who is by a loud

vehicle, music, or even over a phone with a bad connection can be detrimental to communicating effectively. If you have experienced this type of situation, you know how hard it was to hear the speaker, and you had to have them repeat themselves constantly. If you can't fully hear the speaker, essential pieces of the messages can get missed. Other distractions in the workplace could be people near you having separate conversations, people talking and passing by, phones ringing, or even sending an email or typing a document when someone is listening to you. If you find yourself in this situation, stop what you are working on, face the person speaking, and give them your full attention, or walk to a conference room or quiet corner so excessive noise isn't hindering the communication efforts.

When my daughter wants to have a conversation with me and I am working, she often says, "Mom, what's more important me or the computer." It's really cute and gets my attention. When she points this out, I remove the distraction of the computer and I am able to give her my undivided attention.

Acknowledge the speaker

One great thing to do to ensure successful communication is to acknowledge the speaker when they are addressing you. Something as simple as nodding your head or saying yes or I agree can go a long way to let the speaker know you are listening. There is nothing worse than talking to a person who isn't listening or is completely quiet. While some might say that being quiet is polite when someone is talking, it can be taken as disinterested or spacing out. Personally, when I don't get any kind of a response from the listener, I ask if they are listening (or if over the phone, ask if they are still there). Just remember to do this sparingly and to not interrupt the speaker, as that can have negative effects on communication.

I always nod my head or say yes when I am in a conversation with someone. Sometimes, if it's appropriate I will ask clarification questions as well. I always get a better response from the person I am communicating with if I show I am interested in what they have to say. If I don't do this when talking with my daughter, she thinks I am not listening to her.

Take responsibility

Finally, it is significantly important as the listener to take responsibility. Communication can only be as great as the end result, and that is reliant on the role of the receiver just as much as it is on the sender. Both sides need to take responsibility in their role of communication. As the listener, you can be proactive in finding information and listening to messages that are given to you. If you are not getting the information you need, take a close look at the communicator to see if messages are getting sent, but take an even closer look at yourself to see if you are doing everything you need to do to receive the messages.

When communicating with my daughter, I need to make sure I am taking responsibility when I listen. If I don't she will come back to me and tell me I didn't do something she asked me to do. Because I do not want my eight-year-old to be disappointed in me by not following through on something that was asked, I take responsibility as the listener and make sure I am getting all the information I need.

Think about it

1. How can you get your audience to take responsibility in receiving the messages you are sending?
2. How will you build trust with your audience?

Activity

Develop a plan and process for each of the three ways (feedback, metrics, action) you will know if messages were received successfully.

6 GETTING TO KNOW YOU

What does it mean to know your audience? Do I mean know their name, where they live, and what they do for a living? In a sense, yes – all of these pieces of information are good to know about your audience. Companies need to know whom their audience is in order to effectively communicate with them.

You might ask, "What do you mean by 'audience?' I am not a stage in a room full of people - I am a business trying to sell a product or a service to customers." If you think this way, try changing the way you think. Your customers are your audience, and you need to think of them as such. Instead of being gathered in a room, with all eyes on you and having their undivided attention, you have customers scattered across the city, state, country, and even the globe. They are all doing different things, have different needs, and communicate differently. As a business owner and communicator, it is your job to figure out who your target audience is, what they need and want, and how you can reach them. If you know who is buying your products as it makes it easier to communicate effectively with them. You will be able to send a message to them because you know where they spend time – which could be a physical place, online or in another type of media.

While the words (and information) you have are important, it is equally vital to focus on how and why you are saying those words, as are the actual words. Think of it this way: you might tell a toddler and a teenager the same message, but the ways in which you address them are very different. You would not talk to a toddler the same way you would talk to a teenager and vice versa. In the business world, you need to know your audience in the same way and speak with them in a way they will relate to and understand, or your words are useless.

Just because we are all adults, doesn't mean that we will all receive messages the same way. To truly get to know your audience, you must study and then analyze them and their needs and wants. Once you know your audience you can determine your messaging and tactics. This is a very important step in marketing and is often skipped or rushed through. If you spend a little more time and money upfront, your return on investment will be greater.

Your target audience is a very specific type of person. It could be women between the ages of 25-40 who have young children at home, or it could be teenagers who like to skateboard. Once you discover who your target audience is, it will be easier to know what your audience wants and how you can reach them. You can determine who your target is based on the product or service you are selling. If you have a storefront, you can determine your target audience by who is walking into your store. Start a tally and see what the largest group of people is, and then focus on them. If you don't have a storefront, you could try determining who your audience is by reviewing sales and seeing if your target audience is located in the same area, if they are mostly men or women, etc. If you are just starting out and have no customers yet, you could send out a survey to a large group of people to gather information and decide whom your target audience is. Chances are your target audience won't be everyone, and it will be difficult to communicate effectively if your audience is not narrowed down and specific.

Once you know who your target audience is (it may be two different groups of people), you can focus your efforts on studying them, finding out where they hang out, what they like to do, etc. If you find that you have two different groups of people for your target audience, you will likely have two different campaigns going to reach both audiences.

Let's say you are selling cereal and you want to target children and their mothers. You would want the cereal to be enticing to children so you might focus on cartoons or cute animals that would attract the attention of children. This is important so the children ask for the cereal, however they won't be the ones purchasing the cereal, so you also have moms as an audience. You will want to create a campaign that will attract the attention of the mother by focusing on the nutritional and possibly even price point of the cereal.

Again, surveys are a great way to reach a lot of people in a fairly short amount of time and gather a lot of quantitative data. You can use an agency that handles surveys, or you can choose to create and analyze them yourself. There are also a number of online options if you choose to go that route, such as SurveyMonkey, Google Forms, and SurveyGizmo.

Another really great way to know your audience is to go to them. If they hang out at a certain store, coffee shop, or park, go there and watch them from afar, studying their habits and making notes. Talk to them, ask them questions, and get to know their style of communication and what motivates them. You will be surprised at how much information you can gather with interactions like this, and you can also promote your products to the very people who will buy them.

Lastly, the best way to know your audience is to become your audience. Sometimes this is very hard to do; after all, you can't make yourself become a teenager or a toddler again. But you can start doing the same things as your audience, hanging out in the same places, befriending them, and soon you will become your audience and automatically think like them. If you are your target audience it will make it so much easier to be able to communicate and message effectively.

A company who isn't quite sure who their audience is can have the best message in a number of places, but it does no good because it's not speaking to the right people. I have seen this happen time and time again with companies that could be much more successful than they are because they aren't sure who their target audience is. Here's another great example of a company not knowing whom their audience is.

When my daughter was about two years old, I was grocery shopping and buying milk. I reached for a carton that I wanted to buy because I was educated on the company and knew their milk was high quality, and they were environmentally responsible. My daughter however did not want that milk because the packaging was not attractive. Instead she wanted the milk with the cartoon cow on it. I had to search on the carton I was buying to find a cow, so I could show it to my daughter. I bought the milk that I wanted to buy, but that scenario has never left my mind, what if I had not been educated on the company, I would have bought the other milk because my daughter wanted it, and the other company would have lost the sale. That company has now undergone a study to know their audience and changed the look of their packaging to be much more inviting to children, and sales increased by 20 percent after the packaging was updated.

Knowing your audience, or customer, is just one of the steps to effective communication. As you have learned, you must narrow down your audience and focus on a specific group to enhance your communication efforts. If you aren't reaching the right people with the right message in the right place, your time and energy get wasted, and your money will be wasted too!

Think about it

What is your favorite brand? Why do you like it? Think about what makes the brand connect with you.

Activity

Write down who your audience is. What are the demographics? What do they like? Where do they hang out? Develop a good sense of your audience and their needs in this activity, as it will help you greatly with your communication efforts.

7 INTERNAL COMMUNICATIONS

Communication efforts should be about more than what information is getting out to the public. In business, we get so consumed with communicating to our customers that we can neglect our internal stakeholders: the employees. Internal communications is a vital part of a business' success. Employees are our first brand ambassadors and represent the company when out in public on a daily basis. It is important to communicate with them to develop relationships that foster support and understanding of the brand and what the company stands for. If your employees aren't happy, it will show in their daily interactions outside of the office. It can also, and does, affect employee morale inside the office.

There are three types of internal communication efforts to focus on:

1. Communicating down
2. Communicating across
3. Communicating up

Communicating down

When you communicate down, management is taking information and giving it to employees. When deciding what to communicate to employees, you should think transparently. Being transparent and letting employees know of initiatives, projects, and changes before they happen will develop satisfied employees. If you wait to communicate these things until they are already happening or even after they happen, it can generate resentment among the staff. Even if the news isn't the best, employees will appreciate the information sooner rather than later.

Whenever I take my daughter to the park or anywhere else that's really fun and hard to leave, I always give her warnings before we leave. I usually start with a 10-minute warning and then a five-minute warning. When she knows the fun is going to come to an end ahead of time, she takes the news much easier than if I just tell her we are leaving right now. It gives her time to prepare herself mentally for something she doesn't want to do. This is the same for employees; they need time to mentally prepare for something that might not be so fun.

I have seen companies ignore issues and watch secrets by the water cooler get out of control, just because management isn't ready to share information. Sometimes it's because they don't know what's going to happen next, and other times it's because they are afraid of employees' reactions, but regardless of the reason, information is formally withheld, while informally spread like wildfire. Rather than appearing like you are hiding something and being super secretive about it, find the best way to let information out formally as soon as possible. This will create a sense of trust and respect that will go a long way, regardless of the nature of the information.

When deciding the best vehicle to use when communicating with employees, it is important to know the industry and what type of communication vehicles your employees use most. It would be pointless to use email as the primary communication vehicle if your employees are in a warehouse all day and don't get a chance to sit down and check email on a computer or phone. Put some thought into what makes the most sense and why.

Communicating across

Employees need to communicate with each other to get their jobs done. Communicating across can be from manager to manager, co-worker to co-worker, and from department to department. This is the communication that happens on a daily basis and is usually done via phone, email, or face-to-face. Whether sharing information, alerting departments of changes, or seeking out missing information, communication has to happen between each other to keep a business functioning. What information you share, how you share it, and when you share it are important factors to consider when communicating. Withholding information, whether purposefully or accidentally, can be detrimental to a business.

Communicating up

When employees need to communicate something with their manager, it can be scary and difficult. Employees usually have to communicate something negative, such as an error or mistake, and may choose to not communicate if they are afraid of the consequences. It is equally important to have strong communication efforts when communicating up, as something that affects more than just one department could be happening.

Always have open communication with your employees by providing an open door policy and remaining calm and professional when receiving negative information. This will provide an atmosphere of trust where an employee feels comfortable sharing information and communicating with their superior.

Years ago I worked for a boss who did not take bad news well. If anyone would tell them a product wasn't completed on time, or if a machine stopped working, they would yell and throw things. No one wanted to be around in a situation like that, and no one wanted to be the bearer of bad news. The employees hated coming to work and no one talked to each other. Communication was virtually non-existent which made things worse, since no one knew what the other was doing. Turnover was high and it was hard to recruit new employees to want to work in the department.

Each type of internal communication has a different way of reaching out. With communicating down, it is usually down in large quantities, companywide or department-wide, and determining what tool is important, and you will probably want to choose more than one tool so you reach the greatest number of people. When communicating across or up it is usually done face-to-face, by phone or email and as it is usually a more personal interaction because the audience isn't as large since most companywide news comes from the top down.

Remembering the five W's and one H comes in handy when doing any sort of communicating - who, what, where, why, when, and how. Messaging internally is just as important as messaging externally. Review chapter three to find the best way to message internally. Who are you communicating to, what are you communicating, why are you communicating (and why do they care), when are you going to communicate it, and how will you communicate it (what tool(s) will you use). See chapter nine for a more in-depth look at communication tools.

Once you realize the importance of internal communications, you may need help deciding what and how to communicate to employees. Improving your internal communications will improve the overall image of the company internally and externally.

Think about it

Who do you communicate with internally? Could improvements be made in how you communicate with them?

Activity

List the different people or departments that communicate with you and with each other. Write down what they need to know, why they need to know it, how you will get the information to them, when do they need the information, and where will they get the information.

8 EXTERNAL COMMUNICATIONS

Our external communication efforts are so important because it's how the world views and knows your business. Every effort made for external communication should be precise and well thought out, because one wrong move could jeopardize the entire company. Let's look at who external communications reach.

1. Customers
2. Investors
3. Community
4. General public

The list above is a short list and should be customized for your business. Even though the list is short, it is a powerful list.

Customers

Without customers your business wouldn't exist. You
need to communicate effectively with your customers,
so they know what products you have, new products
that are being launched, your company's mission, etc.
There are a number of tools available you can use to
communicate with your customers. Each business is
different, and every one has a different audience to
reach.

Investors

Investors are the people who have invested in your
company and therefore must be communicated with.
Similar to your customers, investors should be
informed about your products, initiatives, and projects.
They would like to know how their money is being
spent and how more money is being made. Investors
generally receive a quarterly newsletter to keep up-to-
date on the business, but they can be communicated to
in a variety of ways.

Community

The community where your business is located should
be remembered when conducting external
communications. While many of the community
members may be your customers, the community

should be focused on a little differently than the rest of your customers. When thinking of communicating with your community, think of what positive things the business is doing. Is it creating more jobs, stimulating the local economy, supporting area schools and clubs? If your company is making a positive impact on your local community, be sure to let the community know.

Living in a rural area, there are a few larger companies who donate to charities and area schools. When these companies do local outreach, the community views them more favorable and they are making a personal connection and show they care about the community instead of just profits for their business.

General public

Similar to the community, the general public may include customers and investors; however, the way you communicate with the general public is very different than how you would communicate with your customers and investors. The general public has an idea of your business, they have heard of you, but they may not be your customers. They may also not be in the community where you are located; however, you should not ignore the general public. When communicating with them, you will want to think big picture. Your reputation is what you should focus on, and ideally you will have a good reputation with the general public. News stories about what you did for your local community or how your product benefited someone in need are always great ways to reach the general public to promote the image of your company.

In the next chapter, you will learn about communication tools so you can determine which tool(s) is right for you and your customers.

Think about it

Why is it necessary to communicate outside your company? Who benefits most from the communication?

Activity

List all the external stakeholders you communicate with. Write down what they need to know, why they need to know it, how you will get the information to them, when do they need the information, and where will they get the information.

9 COMMUNICATION TOOLS

Regardless if you are communicating internally or externally there are numerous communication tools at your fingertips. It is up to you to decide which ones to use and when to use them to get the desired response.

While every company will have a customized list, this list is generalized and designed to give you a place to start. You should add or delete as necessary to effectively communicate as needed.

1.   Email
2.   Meetings
3.   Social media
4.   Intranet
5.   Website

6. Newsletters
7. Webinars
8. Videos

Email

Email is a great communication tool. Nearly everyone has it, its easy to use, quick, and saves paper. Unfortunately there are cons to using email as well. In a company I previously worked for it was one of the most overused tools and was often discredited and overlooked. If email is used sparingly and thoughtfully, it has a better response than when overused. When turning to email for an effective communication tool, you have to ask yourself if any other communication would be more appropriate to use instead. When email is overused it can turn into white noise, and unless someone is expecting an email from you with specific information in it, it might get overlooked or deleted upon receipt. Almost everyone I talk to say they receive too many emails, however they prefer email to other communication vehicles.

So when should you use email?

1. Use email if your recipient has specifically asked to receive information via email.

If you have an email list you maintain where people can subscribe or unsubscribe and have listed email as their preferred method of contact. Alternatively if you have a coworker who is never at their desk and really busy, email might be their preferred method of contact so they can get to it when convenient for them.

2.   Use email if you have short snippets of information.

If you are going to write a short novel, think twice if email is the best tool to use. I know that when I get a really long email, I am tempted to put off reading it. Bulleted lists are great for emails so people can quickly skim and get the main points. Leave the fluff out of emails.

3.   Use email when providing a link to something or giving a call to action.

If you have a link to your website or another website (an article, survey, etc.), send an email so the person can quickly go to the page of reference. If you are asking the recipient to do something, send an email and make sure the call to action is listed in the subject line. That way the recipient can return at a later date and still have all the necessary information needed to complete the requested task.

4. Use email if you want to reach several people at once and no other tool would be appropriate.

While this one is pretty self-explanatory, I will elaborate some. Let's say you have a department or a couple of departments that you need to reach out to and the information is pretty straightforward and to the point. A meeting wouldn't make sense and neither would the other tools, so you send out an email.

Of course, every situation is unique, so follow these guidelines loosely while using your best judgment on what is most appropriate.

Meetings

Meetings are probably my least favorite tool on this list. I pretty much despise meetings. Don't get me wrong, there can be and are some very productive meetings, and sometimes they are necessary; however, most of the time they are not necessary and a waste of time. Use your best discretion when determining if a meeting is absolutely necessary. I have been to more unproductive meetings than I can count. Typically the facilitator (or person who called the meeting) rambles on and on, while the rest of the attendees are either distracted by emails on their laptop or by the unrealistic amount of work to do waiting for them back at their desk. People don't pay attention, forget what was said the minute it leaves the speakers mouth, and feel anxiety about all the work they are not getting done while sitting in a meeting.

If you are forced to sit through a boring meeting, there are some things you can do to help you pay attention. Taking notes is always good to do, when you want to stay focused and remember what was said. You could ask questions to help you understand the points the speaker is trying to make. This can also be done to ensure that you are a necessary participant in the meeting. Making eye contact with the speaker helps you focus during a meeting and shows the speaker you care about what they have to say.

Avoid meeting overload at all costs.

1.   Don't schedule them when not needed.

2.   Avoid inviting unnecessary attendees.

3.   Have an agenda and stick to it.

4.   Know the purpose of the meeting and state it at the beginning. That way if anyone doesn't think it's important to him or her, they can excuse themselves. (You should condone and encourage your employees to do this. They should make the best use of their time, and if a meeting isn't applicable to them, they should be at their desk being productive).

If meetings are limited and productive, employees will appreciate them, and they will benefit communication efforts. If they are overused and a waste of time, employees will resent them and avoid going to them at all costs. They also will hamper your communication efforts and decrease employee morale.

Social Media

Social media is very popular right now and can be beneficial to your company. There are times when you should use social media and times when you should not. I would advise against using social media for internal communications. It's not really an effective tool internally and can cause problems instead of helping communication efforts. I can't think of a reason why social media would be necessary to communicate internally. Social media can be very distracting and a huge time suck, and when communicating internally you want communications to be efficient. Social media can also cause problems if someone posts something inappropriate or offensive.

Using social media as a communication tool when your audience is other businesses is tricky. It depends on a number of things, including what your business does/sells, what the other businesses do, etc. There will be times when it makes complete sense to use social media when communicating to another business and times when it does not. Some sites are better suited to interact with other businesses, so it would make sense to use sites such as Twitter, Google+ and YouTube. Use your best judgment when determining the needs of your business. For the most part, communicating with a business via social media probably isn't the best option and may be a waste of time, but I don't want to say you should never do it.

Social media is a really great communication tool if you want to communicate with the general public. There are so many different sites to choose from, the task can be daunting just thinking about it. Facebook, Twitter, Instagram, Pinterest, Google +, the list goes on and on. What is the best site to be on? This depends on your services/products and your audience. You may begin to wonder if you have time to maintain one or more sites. Depending on how dedicated you want to be with posting and how engaged you want to be with your audience, you may need to hire someone dedicated to these efforts.

Social media can spread the word about your business or products quickly and reach a large number of people if you do it right. Promotions and products are the best things to communicate using social media, but the list is endless with opportunities.

I know personally, when I see a promotion that say click like, share and comment to win something I really want, I do it. My friends and family do as well. Who doesn't want to win something? When companies run promotions like that, the word travels fast and the amount of impressions made increase. It's a good way to increase brand awareness quickly.

Intranet

The intranet is a great way to communicate internally. Most medium to large sized businesses have an intranet, a website dedicated to staff. Typically a password is needed to access the intranet, as it is for employee use only and generally contains confidential information. Depending on the capabilities of your intranet, you can use it to view announcements, provide information about the company, such as HR documents, talking points, product information, etc. Intranets can also host employee specific social media sites, discussion forums, and classified ads. When communicating with employees, an intranet is a good tool, as it can reach nearly all employees and is available 24/7. Other communication efforts might only take place during business hours, but if employees can access information during late shifts or if they are working late at night, they are more likely to see the information. Information is easily accessible and is ready immediately. The downsides to using the intranet to communicate are since not everyone has access to it (employees in the warehouse or driving, not desk jobs), people may forget it's there and miss valuable information or also forget their login information. It should be updated regularly to stay up-to-date as this encourages people to visit regularly. If the information is stagnant and nothing new is posted, employees will lose interest quickly.

Website

Using the website as a communication tool is very similar to using the intranet, except you would use it to communicate with the public or your customers instead of internally. The information here will not be confidential, so it will vary from the information on the intranet. Company information including mission and history are good to put on the website, so your customers know a little about you and how you got to be here. Product and service information is very important to have on the site, as well as locations to buy your products and services. Promotional campaigns, contact information, and any other information that would be of interest to your customers should be here, as well as links to your social media pages so your fans can follow you.

Typically a website will contain a lot of general information about the company and products that aren't constantly changing, but there should also be fresh content added on a regular basis so customers stay engaged and want to keep coming back for new information, whether it be new products that are launching or information about events that you are a part of or other initiatives.

Newsletter

A newsletter can be an effective communication tool internally and externally. A good way to communicate with your employees is to provide regular updates (either monthly or quarterly) via a newsletter. Employees know when and where to expect information, and companies can keep track of when they announced new information. Newsletters can be printed and distributed to employee mailboxes, emailed, or hosted on the intranet. There are a number of options in how to distribute the newsletter, and you should choose the one that makes the most sense for you and your employees.

When sending out a newsletter to your customers, it typically is because you have established a closer relationship with them or they have signed up to receive information from you. Rewards program members, loyal, and long-time customers would all benefit from receiving a newsletter. Again, this would be a regularly published communication (typically quarterly, but could be monthly) and announcements, updates, and any other information you want to share would be included. When communicating externally it is very important to get the receiving preference, so you are not upsetting customers with a piece of mail they would rather receive via email or by visiting your website.

It is important to note here, that while newsletters can be and are effective communication tools, just like everything else they must be used in moderation. If your company has a different newsletter for every department and multiple forms, companies can suffer from newsletter overload, just as they can from meeting or email overload. Choose your newsletters carefully and your content strategically, and they will serve their intended purpose.

Here is a sample layout of a newsletter:

The Water Cooler

Your weekly company update

New Product Launch

We have a new product that will be launching on May 29, 2015. The product will solve all your problems and you will not want to miss it. We will be showing it to employees at the companywide meeting on April 18. If you have any questions or would like to test the product, please attend the meeting. All questions will be answered at that time.

Meetings:

4/15   Marketing/Sales

4/16   Food Service

4/17   Communications

4/18   Companywide

Sales update

The sales department has a new manager. Joe Smith will be overseeing all retail sales and will be stationed at our Alberta office. If you see Joe around the office, please stop to introduce yourself. Joe will be meeting with Marketing in May.

Video

Videos are becoming more and more popular as ways of communicating and can be used in both internal and external communication efforts. Instead of reading something and skipping half the words or missing out on the emotional context of it or reading into something too much, a video can be a compelling tool to use. You can get your message out, it saves your audience time in reading something, and can have strong emotions attached to it. When sending out a serious or exciting message, consider using video instead of print. Video can express emotions in a way that written words cannot and could be more meaningful.

Video can be used in conjunction with other communication tools, such as email, your website, or intranet and social media. They can be long or short, but if using on social media, they should be on the shorter side. You can have how-to tutorials, messages, or fun, interactive videos to gain popularity and increase brand awareness. When done correctly a video can be quite powerful.

Webinar

Webinars can be used both internally and externally and can be live or recorded for later viewing. They are convenient for internal use if your staff is located at more than one location and you have documents you want to share. They are also useful if everyone can't attend at the same time, since they can be recorded and viewed at a later date.

You would want to use a webinar for your customers when you have something to teach them. It might be how to use a new product, such as a sewing machine or kitchen appliance. They can also be used for trainings so your employees can improve customer service skills, email etiquette or mandatory trainings like safety for OSHA. Webinars are great for educational purposes. You could show how to test the soil in your garden or how to use excel, via a webinar.

You can provide your audience, either internal or external, with a link to the webinar if it's live, and if it's recorded you can post to the intranet or website.

The nice thing about webinars being recorded is you can create a library of information to be used in the future without having to recreate meetings or training sessions and can therefore save the company time and money.

Think about it

Does your company have any communication tools that weren't covered in this chapter?

Activity

List all the tools you would use for internal and external customers and when it would be appropriate to use them.

10 CUSTOMER SERVICE

Two of the most important aspects of a successful business are communication and customer service. While they are often focused on individually, you will see that they are closely linked, and it's difficult to have really good customer service without having exceptional communication.

There is an incredible amount of competition between businesses today. Competition is good for your customers, as it helps keep costs down and gives people choices. Competition for businesses means you must stand out from the crowd to be successful. How can you draw your customers in and pull them away from the competition? Having great products is important, but having great customer service is a must.

No matter who your customer is, whether they are a first time shopper or have been around for years, if they are an individual or business, they all deserve to be your number one priority. At a job I previously had, the company used a certain vendor for a service, and the customer service was top notch. They were friendly, always got our requests fulfilled right away, even the last-minute rush jobs, and even though their prices were a little higher than some others around, it was worth it for the customer service they provided. Then they were bought out, and everything changed. We didn't know anyone who worked there, so when we called, we didn't get the friendly hello and chitchat. No one knew anything about our previous orders, so we couldn't refer back to them for duplication; orders were late, not accurate, and it didn't seem like anyone cared that we were having all sorts of issues. After numerous conversations and requests for changes, we finally decided it was time to find a new vendor. In our search, customer service was our number one priority, not cost.

Because most people will pay a little bit extra for exceptional customer service, it should be a goal of your organization to provide the best possible customer service. This chapter will help you develop a customer service strategy centered on communication to help retain and grow your loyal customer base.

Improve your communication and see a greater level of customer service and happier, loyal customers.

First, I want you to think back to a time that you had a positive customer service experience. Undoubtedly you were experiencing great communication on some level. An employee went above and beyond what was expected and told you some really valuable information – perhaps an additional discount was available or a superior product was on sale. These little tidbits of information can go a long way in customer service.

Now think about a time you had a terrible customer service experience. What was the communication like? Was there information missing or late? Was the information presented to you adversely? If you changed the negative aspects of the communication, would your customer service experience have been better? Chances are the answer is yes.

One of the worst customer service experiences I had was when I was purchasing a dishwasher. I was told the appliance would arrive on a certain date and I received an automated call a day before it was supposed to arrive that said it would be another week. A day before it was supposed to arrive for the second time, I got another automated call saying it wouldn't arrive for another four weeks. Since these were automated I wasn't able to talk to anyone. When I tried calling the company, I got a list of numbers to press and none of them fit my needs. When I finally was able to talk to someone, they were in another country and couldn't understand me and told me to call the number I had just called and press a different number. I finally called the store directly where I had to leave a message and waited a few days and no one returned my call. So I had to call back and they wanted me to talk to the manager but they weren't available so I had to leave a message. In all of this, my ordered ended up getting deleted!

There was so much wrong with this experience and it all boiled down to communication or lack thereof. It would have been a much better experience if I was given the actual date of arrival at the beginning or if an actual person would have called and explained why the date was being changed instead of an automated call.

If you have employees that have any level of customer service in their job description, either internally or externally, and the customer service is lacking, you may need to increase communication skills before you can see an improvement in customer service.

Here are five easy steps to increase communication and improve customer service:

1. Smile
2. Ask
3. Listen (really listen)
4. Repeat
5. Solution

Smile

Everyone knows the first impression is always the greatest, and being friendly is such an important part of customer service, but time and time again customer service agents do not smile. Doing this one small, simple task sets the course for how the rest of the interaction will go and should be encouraged and rewarded at your organization. Even if your customer service agents are primarily on the phone, customers can hear a smile in the sound of the voice, and your agents should practice smiling when answering the phone.

Another great thing about smiling is that a positive attitude is contagious (just as a negative one is). If you encourage your staff to be positive, they will follow your example, and morale will be boosted just from this one simple task.

Tip: Have a team meeting at the beginning of each

shift to get everyone in a good mood. Oftentimes employees can be having a bad day in their personal lives and bring that to work with them. Having positive upbeat team meetings at the beginning of the day can encourage employees to leave their problems at the door. Another thing you could do is have a buddy system, where two employees are paired up and encourage each other throughout the day. If you have a customer service representative who does not smile and refuses to leave their problems at the door, try figuring out what the problem is, have HR talk with them or consider another position for them. Negativity is contagious, and you don't want to bring your whole team down because of one person.

Ask

When a customer approaches you or the phone rings, first smile and then ask important questions to show you care. Asking "How may I help you?" or "What can I do for you?" show the customer you are there for them, that they are the most important person to the business at the moment. Having an employee show they care about the customer and their problem (or maybe it's not a problem at all) means a lot. It will likely result in a positive interaction and outcome, and you will retain the customer and possibly gain new ones through word of mouth advertising, like when the customer tells all their family and friends about the great experience they had with your company.

This step should be practiced in a role-playing scenario during training so that it comes off as genuine. Practicing asking questions to find out what the customer wants is very important, as this doesn't happen naturally and will need to be worked at.

Once the questions are asked to show the customer you care, the next step is probably the hardest step to do properly and needs to be practiced until it's perfected.

Listen (really listen)

This step has the highest likelihood of failing because listening is so hard to do. As stated in chapter five, most of the time when people listen to someone speaking they are not really listening, but rather half-listening to what is being said and half-trying to come up with a response to what the person is saying. That is if you are lucky, most of the time people aren't really listening at all, but rather daydreaming or thinking of all the work they have to do once you are done talking or what they are going to make for supper or the other twenty tasks they have to do after work. To provide really good customer service, employees should be trained in active listening so they can listen to exactly what it is the customer needs, wants, or is trying to say.

To actively listen, employees need to focus on the customer and no one or nothing else. They should stop what they are doing and be present in the conversation. They should acknowledge the customer as they are speaking.

Active listening needs to be practiced over and over again before it can be perfected. Try having employees practice with each other before talking with customers so they have some experience in doing this. It is best to clear one's mind before talking with a customer so you can focus all your attention and thoughts on them.

For more information on listening, please refer to the listening section in chapter five.

Repeat

Part of active listening is repeating back to the customer what you heard them say. This will ensure you gathered all the information correctly and gives the customer a chance to hear what they said again. If any information was received incorrectly, the customer can correct it. If not, they can confirm that you heard everything they said, and you can go on to the next step.

If you need help remembering what they are saying, ask them if it's ok if you jot down notes while they are talking so that you capture everything correctly. It is important you ask permission first, otherwise it could be taken as you not listening and working on something else if they see you writing or typing while they are talking. You can also use a mnemonic system to help you remember what they said, so you may repeat it back to them more easily. For example, if a customer is not happy because they received the wrong food in their order and they want you to correct it, you could remember HFC, which stands for happy, food, correct. Remembering the initials of words is a lot easier than trying to remember ever word that the customer said. They will only want you to remember the important pieces anyway, so using this system is helpful. After you do this for a while, it will get easier, and practicing it is always a good idea.

Solution

You have gathered all the data and confirmed it, so now it is time to provide a solution. This is the final stage of the customer service experience. Depending on the situation, you may have predetermined solutions to provide to customers experiencing problems. The solution should satisfy the customer and be of equal or greater value than the original product (or problem). Once a solution is presented, the customer will determine whether the issue is resolved or not. If the customer is not satisfied with the solution, follow steps 1-4 again until the customer is satisfied.

Remember to always smile and ask caring questions, and the information presented should bring you to a satisfactory solution sooner rather than later.

Work with your employees to implement these five steps. Create a plan for training your employees, and then have them put each step into action. They should practice each step for one full week before moving onto the next step, because it will be easier to work on one step at a time, rather than all five at once. Taking it step-by-step will encourage employees to change, and it will happen more slowly and will be easier to add on after a step is mastered. In just five short weeks, your customer service experience will have improved, and your customers will be loyal, and your sales should increase.

Think about it

What was the best customer service experience you've ever had? What else does that company do well?

Activity

Write down the ways customer service could improve at your company. List the steps you can take so your company can reach that level of customer service.

11 WHAT'S NEXT

Communication happens on so many different levels in our lives that sometimes we don't even know it's occurring. The key is to be aware of communication and to be strategic with your efforts. Taking the time to think about what you will say, how you will say, who you will say it to, and when and where you will say it goes a long way in developing a positive message that is well received.

In this book we covered why you need to communicate, the importance of messaging, getting to know your audience, communication problems and failures, internal and external communications, communication tools, and customer service. Each section should teach you the important aspects you need to build a strategic communication plan.

The most important thing to remember is to find out who your audience is and get to know them. Your audience and how well you know them will ultimately determine your success. From that information you can build up your strategy and figure out the best way to approach messaging and communication efforts.

If you were following along and participating in the *Think about it* and *Activity* sections, you should have a solid communications strategy for your business to follow. If you want to take your communication efforts seriously you need to have resources dedicated to communication, such as time and staff, and you need to have technology in place that aligns with your strategy.

Remember that communication is simple when you have all the parts needed and you take action. Don't be afraid to experiment with things, as trial and error is one of the best ways to learn how to communicate better. If something doesn't work, move on quickly – but, if it does work, stick with it and try to replicate it the next time. Review messaging and get feedback from anyone you can. Constructive criticism will help you become a better communicator and will help your business build its reputation.

Be sure to set aside enough time to effectively communicate and implement the steps to your plan. One of the biggest communication failures is not having enough time. Schedule it in your day so that you remember and because it is important enough to schedule. Remember to allow time for your staff to communicate as well and also encourage them to schedule it into their days.

Check your resources to make sure they are solid. If you need more manpower or tools to implement your plan, budget for them. Take communication seriously, and you will reap the rewards it will provide. If your employees see you taking communication seriously, they will follow and will also respect you.

If after reading this book, you still don't have enough knowledge to create or implement a strategic communications plan – contact me (or any other communications consultant), and I will walk you through it (complimentary with proof of a book purchase).

After a plan is developed and in place, you should always revisit the plan frequently in the beginning, once every week for the first month, and then monthly until you feel comfortable with your communication efforts and their results. Then you should revisit the plan at least once a year. Adjustments will need to be made to stay current and to utilize your resources efficiently. If new products or services are added, make sure you get to know any new customers you might attract. Above all, enjoy the new success you will gain by implementing a strategic communication plan.

When I came into a job to oversee a communications department everything was a mess. The website hadn't been updated for four years, newsletters were going out sporadically and had little content of interest to the audience and no one knew what was happening in other departments. I took control of the situation, redesigned and updated the website so it had content that was important to the audience, got the newsletters on a schedule so the audience (and contributors) knew when to expect them and improved internal communications with a weekly newsletter. With structure and strategy a communication nightmare was turned into a communication dream. The audience raved about the changes and was more engaged, departments started working together and communication was timely and appreciated.

Sample Communications Plan

Communication plan for...

Overall objective of communication plan:.

Audience	Objective	Key Message(s)	Vehicle(s)	Timeline (initial date, frequency)

ABOUT THE AUTHOR

Kristel Keys Running has always had a passion for communications. In high school she wrote for the school paper, which carried onto her college years when she wrote for the university paper.

Kristel has continuously worked in the marketing and communications field and is an expert at strategic planning, messaging, and writing. Her industry experience ranges from manufacturing to retail to food and beverages and everything in between.

Kristel founded and is CEO of Obsidian Link Communications Consulting. She helps businesses identify their communication needs, develops a strategy on how to meet those needs and helps implement the plan, as needed. She also conducts workshops and trainings on best practices in communicating.

Kristel has a bachelor's degrees in Communication Technologies Management and a master's degree in Business Communications. She lives in rural Wisconsin with her husband, Adam, and two small children.